W Polsce też jest
wiele pięknych
miejsc.

Kasina 21.7.2005r.

text

photographs

Olgierd Budrewicz

Tadeusz Budziński

Adam Bujak

Piotr Bułanow

Jan Ciesielski

Robert Dejtrowski

Jerzy Habdas

Adam Hawałej

Janusz Leśniak

Ryszard Nater, Zygmunt Nater

Paweł Pierściński

Andrzej Raj

Stanisław Składanowski, Bogumiła Piazza

Piotr Skórnicki

Marek Strzałkowski

Jerzy Undro

Piotr Witosławski

Poland

From Sea
to Mountains

BOSz

Graphic design
Władysław Pluta

Editor
Joanna Kułakowska-Lis

English translation by
Teresa Bałuk-Ulewiczowa

DTP
BOSZ, Maciej Haudek, Iwona Pieniak

Pre-press
JML, Jacek Jutrzenka, Warszawa

Printing
Gorenjski Tisk, Kranj – Slovenija

Publisher
Wydawnictwo BOSZ
Olszanica 2005

First edition

© Copyright by BOSZ

ISBN 83-89747-13-8

Photographs
Tadeusz Budziński
page 158, 159, 160–161, 162, 163, 164, 165, 166–167,
176–177

Adam Bujak
page 74, 88–89, 132–133, 134, 135, 152, 153, 156–157

Piotr Bułanow
page 57, 58–59, 60g, 62g

Jan Ciesielski
page 9, 41, 48, 49, 50–51, 52, 53, 54, 55, 56

Robert Dejtrowski
page 169

Jerzy Habdas
page 90, 91, 92, 93

Adam Hawałej
page 120, 121, 122, 123

Janusz Leśniak
page 144, 145, 146, 147, 150

Ryszard Nater, Zygmunt Nater
page 137, 170, 171, 172–173, 174, 175

Paweł Pierściński
page 100–101, 102, 103, 106, 107, 108, 109, 110, 111, 112,
113, 114–115, 116, 117, 118–119

Andrzej Raj
page 124, 125, 126–127, 128, 129, 130, 131

Stanisław Składanowski, Bogumiła Piazza
page 14–15, 20, 21, 22, 23, 24, 25, 26, 27, 28, 29, 30–31,
32, 33, 34, 35, 36–37, 38, 39, 42g, 45, 46, 47, 73, 75, 76, 77

Piotr Skórnicki
page 78, 79, 80, 81, 82, 83, 84, 85, 86, 87

Marek Strzałkowski
page 60d, 61, 62d, 63, 64, 65, 66, 67, 68–69, 70, 71, 96, 97

Jerzy Undro
page 16, 17, 18–19, 42d, 43, 44

Piotr Witosławski
page 94, 95, 98, 99, 105, 138, 139, 140, 141, 142, 143, 148,
149, 151, 154, 155, 178, 179, 180–181, 182–183, 184, 185,
186, 187, 188, 189, 190–191

BOSZ

38-622 Olszanica 311
Office: 38-600 Lesko, ul. Parkowa 5
tel. +48 (13) 4699000
tel./fax +48 (13) 4696188
e-mail: biuro@bosz.com.pl
www.bosz.com.pl

Poland

Olgierd
Budrewicz

Poland
From Sea
to
Mountains

The British historian Norman Davies entitled one of his books on Poland *Heart of Europe*. In his account of the history of this country and nation he turned his attention to time and place, as a specialist in the field would be expected to do. His description of the course of events and the fate of the people living on this historically none too tranquil territory does not shy away from emotions and subjective, but on the whole accurate assessment, as in the last sentence of its Polish translation: "The Poles are the world's masters in the art of survival."

For centuries the lands between the Oder and the Bug, and formerly also those further east, were the setting of dramatic events. It's worthwhile trying to answer at least briefly what that setting – that Heart of Europe – is like today.

Let's start with the Vistula.

The River Vistula is not another Amazon, Nile, Mississipi, or Ganges. It's just a bit over 1,000 km long. But is a river's length its decisive feature? Sometimes grand events are played out on the banks of modest rivulets. "The River Vistula flows across the Polish lands," says the song. It dissects Poland from north to south, it's like the country's backbone. A symbol of the Polish State. "Just as the Vistula will never cease to flow, so will Poland never perish," say the words of another song. The Vistula is mentoned in the Polish national anthem, and in countless songs and poems, proverbs and sayings. It's still not been fully regulated, so sometimes it's called Europe's last romantic river.

Many historic, important towns and cities lie along the Vistula's banks, to mention but Cracow, Sandomierz, Puławy, Dęblin, Warsaw, Płock, Toruń, and Gdańsk.

Much has happened along these banks. A major trading route ran here. They are dotted with battlefields ancient and modern. Events that occurred in Cracow, Warsaw, or Gdańsk decided the country's future.

Let's start with Cracow. Without this royal city there'd be no Poland today. To quote the writer Tadeusz Boy Żeleński, in Cracow we still have the very much alive "legend of this city of painters, poets, grand tombs and stained glass, this city of life and art." It's the Florence of Central Europe: a place full of magic, its landmark Wawel Hill pinnacled

by the mighty Castle; with the Czartoryski Museum, home of "The Lady with the Ermine," Poland's only Leonardo; with its delightful Market Square and the crowds admiring the Cloth Hall and St. Mary's Church with the Veit Stoss Altar, listening to the bugle-call from the church-tower. On special days the sonorous peal of the Sigismundian Bell resounds from the Cathedral.

It must have been a miracle that Cracow survived the devastation of the Second World War. Almost all the historic sites, not just the monumental works of art and architecture, but also the private houses and Gothic cellars came out unscathed. Even Kazimierz, the Jewish quarter, was saved – an unprecedented fact for Poland.

Today an atmosphere of bygone times still lingers in its narrow streets and lanes – an atmosphere so special you would probably not be too surprised if suddenly Nicolaus Copernicus, Veit Stoss, Jan Kochanowski, Stanisław Wyspiański, or Józef Mehoffer appeared round the corner. Only yesterday you could have met extraordinary personalities here, like Czesław Miłosz (until recently Cracow was a city with 2 Nobel prizewinners; today only Wisława Szymborska is left), or inspired poets, great artists, renowned scholars from the Jagiellonian University, one of Europe's oldest universities. This was the city of Cardinal Karol Wojtyła, John Paul II, the Polish Pope.

"Cracow was not built in a day," says the proverb. But eventually the job was done, and the result is stupendous, as anyone can see. No wonder that anything you see in Poland after Cracow will seem humbler, not so valuable, not so beautiful.

Even if the odd work of art survived in Warsaw, only a bighead would venture on comparing the sights of the capital with Cracow's Wawel Hill, Barbakan, Florian Gate, or the innumerable churches built here in diverse styles and times.

Historic sights are not what Warsaw is famous for. The extraordinary thing about Warsaw is its intransigent, patriotic stance at the moment of truth. What's really amazing is that this city managed to survive its clinical death during World War 2. Destroyed and razed to the ground, turned into a desolate heap of rubble, it found the strength to rise and rebuild itself.

The Vistula, much broader in Warsaw than in Cracow, has played a salient part in the 800 years of Warsaw's history. Its bridges were destroyed on numerous occasions, blown up or swept away by floods. The 1920 Bolshevik offensive was stopped not far from here, and the event rightly dubbed "the Miracle on the Vistula." In 1944 the insurgents of the Warsaw Uprising waited in vain here for assistance from the Soviet troops stationed idly on the other bank.

Though Warsaw could hardly vie with the museums of Cracow, nonetheless much of the old-time charm of the "Paris of Central Europe" lingers on in its numerous palaces and parks, especially the Royal Łazienki Gardens. Warsaw's Old City has been meticulously reconstructed, with a splendid thoroughfare starting from Royal Castle down the Krakowskie Przedmieście, along Nowy Świat and on to Aleje Ujazdowskie. All to dispel the memories of the bad old days and fill the city's new districts with the vigour and hubbub of life, to open up new prospects.

Scores of books have been written on Warsaw, the city that refused to die. Its antique showcases were all crushed, but here they are once again. Brilliant conservation artists came along and as if by the touch of a magic wand reconstructed the old walls and even restored their old-time atmosphere. When there were no plans or even photographs to go by, they used paintings by old masters, especially Canaletto. It was a unique achievement on a world scale. That's why – as in days bygone – you may well hear an echo of Chopin's mazurkas and polonaises rippling through Krakowskie Przedmieście or the Łazienki Gardens.

Every generation of Poles loves Warsaw, city of national uprisings, and scene of many a battlefront. Now that love is maybe more reserved and not as spontaneous as it was just after the War, when the poet Andrzej Nowicki wrote. "If I'm to die, let me perish, For Nowy Świat filled with wreckage."

Poland's capital deserves profound reflection. You need to keep in mind its past and changing people and scenes, and see it as something like a different planet. And definitely keep returning here, to surprise yourself each time by the continual transformations of its landscapes and people, its sounds and colours.

Time now to head north, still along the Vistula, as it winds past cities crouched on its banks, until it finally reaches its estuary. To the Baltic city of Gdańsk, a once renowned Hanseatic port. Here, too, a great history has left numerous vestiges. Its strongest note was struck in the 1980's with the birth of the Solidarity movement and the beginning of Europe's victorious struggle to throw off its political shackles.

In 1939 a French writer asked dramatically though neither prudently nor properly, *"Mourir pour Dantzig?"* Later his words would become the ill-advised politician's and time-server's catchphrase. One-tenth of Gdańsk's fine old town-houses, churches, towers and granaries survived the final phase of the War.

Years passed. The splendid Main Town Hall, Artus' Court, and the Long Market were restored. The painstakingly rebuilt streets and fine interiors could again host the city's erstwhile celebrities – Arthur Schopenhauer, Johannes Hevelius, Gabriel Fahrenheit. Günter Grass, the German Nobel prizewinner who was born here, has written a Gdańsk trilogy, and is an honorary citizen, sometimes pays a visit. You might see a passer-by with a familiar-looking moustache. He smiles when you say, "Hello." It's Lech Wałęsa, who lives here.

On fine days in spring and summer the streets and bars of Gdańsk fill up with young people. In an atmosphere of peace and goodwill you can down a tankard of beer or – if you can afford it – a glass of Goldwasser vodka . . .

Someone might feel we had done an injustice to the cities and towns along the Vistula we'd missed as we sped on our way north – places like Sandomierz, Kazimierz, Puławy, Toruń, or Chełmno.

Sandomierz, which sits on a high escarpment overlooking the Vistula, is almost as old as Poland herself. Ravaged by numerous disasters such as wars and great fires, this town of just 30 thousand inhabitants has still managed to preserve some real masterpieces of religious and secular art. You'll hear stories about the labyrinth of Sandomierz's dungeons and cellars which once held grain, wine, and other commodities, and often harboured fugitives.

Sandomierz was an important cultural centre, with its vintage town-houses and

Who speaks to me of my native land,
Of fields with flowers replete,
Of cots and crofts – all these, he'll understand,
    Lie but at her feet.

Cyprian Kamil Norwid
1821–1883

gates, a key point on trading routes, a place of prosperity attracting settlers from abroad. Today it entices tourists, who admire the ancient houses and look down from the escarpment on to the green fields and loess lands below.

Not far away is the Świętokrzyskie, with mountains of the same name. Many scholars believe this is where the origins of Poland's industries go back to. It all started in the Stone and Iron Ages. From the early Middle Ages there was a metal industry here for the non-ferrous metals: lead, silver, and copper. By the 16th century there were many smithies working here, the remains of which, the hammers and smelting-shops, and even ancient foundries, you can still see today.

This land is famous for its legends, still fresh today but originating in pagan times. If there's any truth in them, the region's full of witches, devils, and ghosts. Some of the stories are associated with real events, especially the wars that harassed the area. Stefan Żeromski, who came from the region, left it a beautiful testimonial in his novels. Another writer, Jarosław Iwaszkiewicz, observed the wonder of the mixes of life and poetry here, the mist-clad hills and moon so like a poem. The forests (though somewhat thinned) still rustle here, and in them the firs, beech-trees, and larches. Along with a celebrated oak, Bartek, perhaps as old as the Polish State. A wonderful, mysterious land. With an extraordinary natural world, but also with ancient Cistercian abbeys, country houses and cottages, castles, roadside shrines, and graveyards of various religions. All surmounted by the old Benedictine Abbey (now an Oblate monastery) at Święty Krzyż (Holy Cross Hill).

We'll whisk back to the Vistula again, to Kazimierz Dolny. The population's just 3 thousand, but in spring when the fruit trees are in blossom there'll be ten times that number here. For years Kazimierz prospered on its riverside granaries, which collected up the grain from the locality, while their proprietors lived in the arcaded Renaissance houses around the marketplace, today favourite photographic subjects for the crowds of tourists who come here.

It's only a stone's throw to Puławy, once the family seat of the aristocratic Lubomirski and Czartoryski, with a stately home set in a romantic landscape park. Puławy was once an important national centre for culture and society life. It later became an industrial town with a nitrogen plant and an agricultural research centre.

Nearby is Dęblin, with the famous School of Young Eagles, which trained the Polish Air Force pilots who made such a heroic contribution to the Battle of Britain.

Now we'll leap-frog Warsaw and land in Toruń, once known as a "little Cracow." This city survived wartime devastation, perhaps looked after from the beyond by Nicolaus Copernicus. It's his birthplace. A statue to commemorate Copernicus was put up in 1853 in Toruń's marketplace with a Latin inscription reading, "To the one who moved the Earth and stopped the Sun." The memory of Copernicus draws the tourists in to Toruń, though the city has far more to offer. For instance its 14th-century town hall and St. Mary's Church, plus a host of other sights, a leaning tower 1½ metres out of the vertical. The 15th-century chronicler Jan Długosz wrote Toruń was a city of exceptional beauty in a wonderful location, and famous for its fine houses and roofs in red brick. In the 16th century it was one of the most prosperous cities in Poland. Today it has over 300 registered historic sites, including Gothic edifices with splendid details on their façades and in the interiors. The Cathedral has a gotic baptismal font in which Copernicus was christened. As you tour Toruń and admire its old-world town-houses and its thick fortification walls, you should be munching some Toruń gingerbread. It's as renowned as its counterparts from Nuremberg and Aachen, and has a flavour of medieval mystery.

You can't get very far away from the Vistula: Poland's hardly imaginable without it. But of course the country has other rivers and regions. With a territory of 312 sq. km, it's bigger than Italy and four times the size of Austria.

Not far from the bend on the Vistula north of Warsaw there is a country of lakes and forests, fish and fowl, one of the most beautiful regions in this part of Europe. Varmia and Masuria offers a world of white sails, black and white swans, hundreds of storks' nests. It's dotted with castles, Gothic and Baroque churches, monasteries, historic guildhalls, small fishing towns and hundreds of holiday centres. The tranquillity has an undercurrent of historic memories. In 1410 a tremendous battle was fought on the field at Grunwald, between the joint Polish and Lithuanian forces against the Teutonic Knights. Ulrich von Jungingen, Grand Master of the Teutonic Knights, was slain. Not far away Gierłoż marks the site of the notorious Wolfsschanze or "Wolf's Lair," Hitler's secret HQ, scene of the unsuccessful attempt to assassinate the Führer in 1944.

Now we head west across the Vistula, to visit a fascinating region inhabited by the Kashubians. They number half a million and have their own language, related to Polish but with many words and grammar structures from some extinct languages. Linguists classify Kashubian in the Lechitic group of the Slavonic languages. It's a similar story with the Kashubian folklore and folk art. The Kashubians have always thought of themselves as Polish, and the cultures have intermingled. You can learn about many of their special features in the open-air ethnographic museum at Wzdzydze Kiszewskie. After all, the Kashubians are a special folk: only in Kashubia do people still take the splendid Polish snuff.

There's so much in Northern Poland! From stately Gdańsk, through modern (interwar) Gdynia, the 35-km snip of the Hel Peninsula, Western Pomerania with Słupsk, Kołobrzeg, and other seaside health resorts, down to Szczecin on the Oder, a busy seaport near the German border. Szczecin prides itself on its Castle of the Dukes of Pomerania, its historic Gothic churches, gates, and houses. The huge devastation of the last World War has been removed – maybe overgrown by the green parks and squares?

Many are the jewels in Poland's crown. On this brief tour we can admire but a few.

The roads south from Szczecin go through charming small-time towns like Łagów, which has a film festival, but also places claiming metropolitan status, like Gorzów Wielkopolski, Zielona Góra, Legnica, Wałbrzych, Wrocław, and Opole.

Well, Wrocław. Mustn't be missed. Capital of Lower Silesia. City of the Piast and Habsburg dynasties, once under Czech and Prussian rule. Since the end of World War 2 the Poles (many from Lwów) have been here again. Wrocław deserves attention and admiration. In 1948 Pablo Picasso saw its dynamic development

as a stimulus to his creativity. After Warsaw, Wrocław is Poland's second miracle of reincarnation. Not just its walls have been lifted up from the ruins. It has witnessed a remarkable development of the arts and sciences. It's the city of Jerzy Grotowski's and Henryk Tomaszewski's world-famous theatres. The city to which the Ossolineum scholarly institution and library transferred from Lwów. Visitors are fascinated by *the Panorama Racławicka*, a huge painting showing the Battle of Racławice (1794), set inside a rotunda. Then there are Wrocław's older sights, all lovingly restored. Their biggest concentration is on Ostrów Tumski Island, with the Cathedral (13th-14th-c.) and magnificent chapels: St. Mary's, St. Elizabeth's, and the Elector's Chapel, along with their peer, the Church of the Holy Cross. There's also Piasek Island, and the marketplace with its Late Gothic town hall, churches, and mansions. The builders and artists of olden times were lavish with their talent and effort. Alas, in 1945 the Hitler's Nazis turned Wrocław into a bastion and signed its death-warrant. It's good that the memory of the ensuing disaster survives, now only in the documentary photographs and scholarly works, and of course in those who saw it with their own eyes.

From Lower Silesia you can continue on to Upper Silesia, a land of industrial chimneys, slag-heaps and social problems like those in the Ruhr or Manchester. Upper Silesia's been dubbed a black country, but it has a green backdrop with delightful health resorts like Wisła, Ustroń, Szczyrk and Jaszowiec.

So let's whip north again, for Częstochowa. A place with an important site dear to all Polish hearts: Jasna Góra Hill. The Monastery perched on it houses the famous Holy Picture of Our Lady of Częstochowa, the Black Madonna. The destination of innumerable pilgrimages from Poland and abroad, Jasna Góra has hosted as many as a million pilgrims all at once. It's had several visits from John Paul II. In 1655 the Monastery was besieged by the Swedes, and its saintly prior, Father Augustyn Kordecki, earned a place in history for its brave defence.

Historically Poland is divided up into Greater and Lesser Poland (Polonia Major and Minor), although delimiting these regions is hard for the average citizen, not to speak of visitors from abroad. Częstochowa lies more or less between Greater and Lesser Poland. Northwest of Częstochowa lies Poznań, capital of Greater Poland. For many centuries Poznań has been a commercial focus, ever since itinerant merchants put it on the Amber Road. It's still a key business centre, since 1925 the venue for the Poznań International Trade Fairs, events of European importance. Poznań's one of Poland's oldest municipalities. Since the 10th century it has seen history in the making, first as Poland's principal urban centre, and from 968 a cathedral town. A stream of events, both good and bad, followed. The city grew and thrived, but its prosperity was interrupted by the Swedish Wars, natural disasters, the struggle to stop Germanisation, the Greater Polish Uprising, Nazi occupation, fighting and damage during World War 2, and the violently suppressed workers' Anti-Communist uprising of 1956. Despite the adversities Poznań has many surviving and restored historic sites, such as its town hall, the mansions in its marketplace (16th-18th c.), the Odwach (guard-house), the municipal weighbridge house, the Baroque Parish Church, and the Cathedral, parts of which go back to the 10th century.

A series of pretty towns, castles, country cottages, and fine gardens and parks lie within a radius of 100 km from Poznań. I'll mention just Rogalin and Kórnik, but they're all well worth a visit.

On this tour it's best to get off the beaten track and go cross-country. So right now we're in Southern, that is Lesser, Poland. Having familiarised ourselves with Cracow, let's stop for a while in reflection at the tragic relics of the Auschwitz concentration camp. To the east of Cracow there's Wieliczka, with one of the world's oldest (10th-century?) and most spectacular salt-mines, a UNESCO World Cultural Heritage site.

What's next? Hundreds of Sub-Carpathian treasures, like the fantastic wooden churches and chapels, most of the 200 very old places of worship of various religions, at Dębno, Sękowa, Przydonica, Binarowa, and many more. Some with glorious polychromies. Fortunately, a few synagogues, Eastern-Rite churches, burial grounds, roadside shrines have managed to withstand the ravages of history.

If you have the time, do look in to the Podhale mountain region, with Zakopane,

Krynica, Nowy Sącz and Stary Sącz. Heading east, you'll come up to the "Eastern Wall," an antechamber to Poland's former Eastern Marches. Starting from the Bieszczady Mountains in the south, along the frontier River Bug, up to Augustów and Suwałki in the north, the region abounds with exotic surprises. The primeval Forest of Białowieża for a start . . . the marshes around the River Biebrza, home to a startling natural world. The Tartar settlement at Krynki. Set off by the Renaissance city of Zamość, designed by Bernardo Morando of Padua. Then the border city of Przemyśl, teeming with Baroque churches. And Łańcut Castle with its Apartments and Carriage Museum, and the music festivals and concerts held there. And right in the north, along the Lithuanian border, you'll see a string of scenic lakes like Hańcza, and the Augustów Canal, a feat of early 19th-century engineering by a team led by Ignacy Prądzyński.

To round off the trip, a word about the extraordinary scenic diversity you'll see in Poland – from the high Tatras to the Baltic dunes. Her natural world is spangled with historic cities, towns, castles, symbols of the past, vestiges of history. In them you'll discover the marks of many cultures, though today's Poland is essentially homogeneous, as never before in her history. Only some of these treasures figure in the guidebooks, you'll have to search for the others yourself, discover and experience them, be amazed and try to understand.

This travelogue barely hints at the other things worthy of notice. I've missed a lot out: the beautifully restored, mighty Teutonic Knights' Castle at Malbork, the ancient town of Wiślica, Pieskowa Skała Castle, Kłodzko, Krasiczyn, Gniezno, Kalwaria Zebrzydowska, Biskupin, Baranów, Kielce, Jędrzejów, Płock, and scores of other exciting places. I've said nothing about national customs – the link binding together the events of history, culture, religion. But give me a chance to write a multi-volume work on our extraordinary country, and I'll show you what I can do!

In the 18th century people in Poland used to say, "God's too high up, and France too far away." When the Second World War was over, which Poland allegedly won, all the Western countries were too far away. For a long time the Yalta arrangements cast a land of free people into a totalitarian system, which luckily was eventually vanquished. For a land whose history has certainly not been blessed with prolonged periods of peace and prosperity, modern Poland offers both its visitors and its people an amazing number of places for tranquil contemplation of the past, leisurely enjoyment of the present, and an opportunity to look forward to the future in an atmosphere of calm expectation. Let's close with the words of Norman Davies, "The Poles are the world's masters in the art of survival."

Olgierd Budrewicz

Olgierd Budrewicz, born in Warsaw in 1923. Writer, traveller, journalist and reporter. Graduate of the Faculty of Law, Warsaw University, and of the School of Journalism. During the Second World War he was a member of the AK Polish resistance force and a combatant in the 1944 Warsaw Uprising. Olgierd Budrewicz has published scores of travelogues and travel books, biographical works and books on Warsaw, which have been translated into many languages and re-issued many times. He holds numerous awards and distinctions.

The Baltic, Poland's sea. The Polish people have fought many wars for access to it;
and when their efforts proved successful they held ceremonies of commitment to their sea.

Szczecin – *an important, historic seaport on the Bay of Szczecin. Once ruled by the mighty Gryfita family of princes, then by Sweden and Prussia, since 1945 Szczecin has belonged to Poland. Now it is a modern city thriving on its frontier and seaboard location*

Szczecin. The Gothic façade of St. Peter's and St. Paul's Church is just round the corner, the Castle of the Dukes of Pomerania is straight ahead, and the Royal Gate is nearby.

The Embankment of Boleslaus the Brave at dusk. This riverside promenade was created in the 19th century on the site of the old Prussian fort.

The entire length of the Oder has been regulated,
and today it is Poland's best navigable
inland waterway.

Grodzka Island in the Oder's main channel. With the Embankment of Boleslaus the Brave, the National Museum, and the Voivodeship Office in the background.

Kołobrzeg Port, a popular Baltic health resort.
A lighthouse stands on the site of an 18th-century fortress.

The 19th-century, Neo-Gothic structure of Ustka Lighthouse stands at the entrance to the port. Its viewing platform offers a magnificent panorama of the locality.

Shifting dunes in the Słowiński National Park, which has been entered on the World Heritage List of biosphere reserves on account of its special natural features.

The coast at Władysławowo, a popular resort at the base of the sandbar on the Hel Peninsula.

23

Lake Żarnowieckie. The local electricity station accounts
for variations of several metres in its water level.

Pomerania (*Pomorze*)
*is a historic land along
the southern Baltic, with
a fascinating, differentiated
landscape sculpted by
the Scandinavian glacier.
The Gdańsk, Central, and
Western parts of Pomerania
offer a stretch of dunes,
beaches, scenic lowlands,
beautiful woodlands,
and places of historic
interest, now the setting
for numerous holiday
resorts.*

Dawn over the woodlands
around Lake Dywan at Sominy.

Chojnice. The towers of the 14th-century Parish Church
and the Baroque Church of the Annunciation.

Sunset over the lake at Łapalice
near Kartuzy in Kashubia.

The primeval part of the Bory Tucholskie forest, the largest stretch of woodland in Pomerania, and one of the largest forests in Poland.

A picturesque river gorge called Jar Raduni.

An artificial gradient drop on the River Radunia,
which has an exciting landscape along its middle and lower course.

Kartuzy Church was once in the hands of the Carthusian Order, famous for its ascetic lifestyle. The roof on this church is in the shape of a coffin, to remind people of the transience of life.

An alcoved house at Salina: a rare specimen of a structure combining two building styles: the traditional Polish country cottage with the Pomeranian post-and-beam technique.

A cottage in the Kluki Open-Air Museum, where you can see what a traditional Słowiny village looked like.

The blacksmith's shop on the Hel Peninsula.
Fishing nets hanging up to dry in the port.

Gdańsk – *a splendid port,*
once a Hanseatic city, full
of mementoes of its turbulent
past. Gdańsk had its heyday
in the 16th and 17th centuries,
when it was Poland's chief port
and largest metropolis.
It was restored to Poland after
World War 2. Today Gdańsk
is once again a delightful sight.

Nepture's Fountain went up in front of Artus' Court in the mid-17th century.
It was founded by the City Mayor.

The Three Crosses Memorial in tribute to the shipyard- and dockworkers
who died in the tragic events of the strike in December 1970.

Artus' Court, trysting-place of Gdańsk's patrician guilds,
has an impressive façade, a foretaste of the opulence of the building's interiors.

The panorama of the old part of Gdańsk (*Główne Miasto*)
is dominated by the massive Gothic Church of St. John.

The 15th-century Gdańsk Crane was used for unloading ships, and was probably the largest device of its kind in Europe. Thanks to its mighty walls it was also a defence structure.

Ulica Mariacka is a street which has preserved
the atmosphere of the old Gdańsk.

Riverside view of the row of houses
in the Główne Miasto (old part) of Gdańsk.

The Main Town Hall of Gdańsk was erected in the Długi Targ (Long Market)
soon after the city was endowed with a municipal charter.

Beautiful land, I cannot but adore you,
Your ancient forests and reedy lakesides;
Cannot but love the sun rising o'er you,
When on your hills its golden plough glides.

Jan Szczawiej
1906–1983

Cape Westerplatte,
*famous for its heroic defence
in September 1939.
The shots fired from the
German battleship
Schleswig-Holstein at this
Polish garrison started the
Second World War.
For seven days the crew
and its commanding officer,
Major Sucharski, withstood
an attack by a German
force that massively
outnumbered them.*

A sailing-ship regatta to mark the millennium of Gdańsk.
The Dar Młodzieży, berthed off the Westerplatte Peninsula.

Waiting for
the wind.

On the crest of a wave. The Baltic off the Polish coast,
especially in the Bays of Szczecin and Gdańsk, offers excellent conditions for sailing.

A sail in harmony with the silhouettes
of the cranes in the Port of Szczecin.

The cranes of the Gdańsk shipyard, famous as the birthplace
of Solidarity, where Poland's democratic transformation started.

Malbork Castle, seat of the Grand Master of the Teutonic Knights, erected in the early 14th century, with later redevelopments. The largest Gothic fortress in Europe.

The Gothic structure of Frombork Cathedral and the fortifications testify to the history of this city, where Nicolaus Copernicus spent his last years.

Elbląg harbour. Ships set off from here along
the Elbląg Canal to Ostróda. There is a sharp gradient on the way,
with several locks and gradient drops.

The Gothic Church at Orneta is regarded as one of the most interesting churches in Varmia (*Warmia*).

The monumental Parish Church of St. John, Kętrzyn.

The Gothic edifice of Olsztyn Castle,
once the seat of the chapter of the Diocese of Varmia.

Evening on Lake Luterskie near Jeziorany. This land invariably casts
its spell on artists, poets and ordinary folk alike.

The Pasłęka, second largest river in Varmia and Masuria, winding its way to the Bay of the Vistula.

The reserve of the Łyna River Source is one of the few source-water areas in Poland open to the public.

The emblem of the Masurian Natural Landscape Park is a white stork, and for good reason.
Here you'll see the famous "stork villages", with a nest up on virtually every roof and tree.

Masuria (*Mazury*),
Land of a Thousand Lakes,
a tourist region of exceptional
beauty. You can hardly fail
to be spellbound by its
forests, meandering rivers,
moraine hillocks, and
its magnificent wildlife,
as well as by the numerous
historic sites – Gothic
churches and Teutonic castles,
which spill over into
neighbouring Varmia
(Warmia).

There are thousands of lakes in Masuria,
making the region a boater's paradise.

Lake Limajno,
near Dobre Miasto.

Swans are a common sight in Masuria.
Their largest colony in Poland lives on the reserve near Lake Łuknajno.

56

Masuria, especially its eastern part, is a land of long, cold winters
with lots of snow. Temperatures drop to well below
zero Centigrade, but oh, the sights!

A wooden cross in the village of Sobolewo. Poland's eastern edges are home to many cultures and religions.
The inhabitants include Catholics of the Roman and Byzantine (Ukrainian) Rite, Eastern Orthodox Christians,
Old Believers of the Pre-Nikon Russian Orthodox Church, and Muslims.

Scenic Lake Jeglówek, one of the post-glacial Szurpilskie Lakes. Northern Poland
is the best part of the country for a variety of post-glacial topographical formations.

Kurzyniec Lock on the Augustowski Canal, constructed in 1828.
The Canal is an Industrial Revolution heritage site, unique in its class in Europe.

Lake Szurpiły has an irregular,
partly afforested shoreline.

On the Czarna Hańcza. This river is one of Poland's best-known,
most scenic canoeing courses.

Podlassia (*Podlasie*)
*is a trysting-ground where
East meets West, with
Eastern-Rite Orthodox
and Uniate churches,
and even Tartar mosques;
with the rustling Forest
of Białowieża, and the
wildfowl nestling on the
marshes around the River
Biebrza. This still virgin
countryside carries
a nostalgic air of the
former Borderlands.*

The old monastic buildings of the Camaldolese Hermitage
near Lake Wigry in the Augustów Lake District.
The beautiful surroundings must certainly have inspired contemplation.

The Renaissance/Baroque
Dominican Church
and Monastery at Sejny.

The 18th-century mosque at Kruszyniany,
a Tartar village in Podlassia (*Podlasie*).
The Tartar community has lived here for the past three hundred years.

Grabarka Hill, a holy mountain and place of pilgrimage for Eastern Orthodox Christians.
It's a tradition for pilgrims to set up their individual penitential crosses here.

Poland's eastern edges are full of Orthodox and Byzantine-Rite Uniate churches, both the old wooden ones, as well as brand new edifices – like Hajnówka Church.

The Białowieża Forest, one of Europe's last surviving stretches of natural virgin forest.

The Bison, emblem of the Białowieża National Park.

The yellow lady's slipper (*Cypripedium calceolus, American Valerian*) is a wild orchid under full protection and grows in the forests of north-eastern Poland.

Cottages in the village of Saczkowce, in the row arrangement typical for this frontier
part of Poland, where time seems to have stopped . . .

A cottage in the open-air museum at Budy
near Białowieża.

A potter proudly presents his wares.
Authentic folk crafts still survive in some places.

An angler on the River Bug
near Mielnik.

Of you, ivy-wrapped walls, I'm fonder and fonder,
For the sight of those moss-clad roofs ever yearning,
While the sad, grey Vistula rustles by yonder,
Through lonesome eyes thoughts run back returning.

Or-Ot
Artur Oppman
1867–1931

Płock Cathedral perched high on an escarpment over the Vistula. Płock is one of the oldest cities in Mazovia (*Mazowsze*). For a spell in the 11th century it even served as Poland's capital.

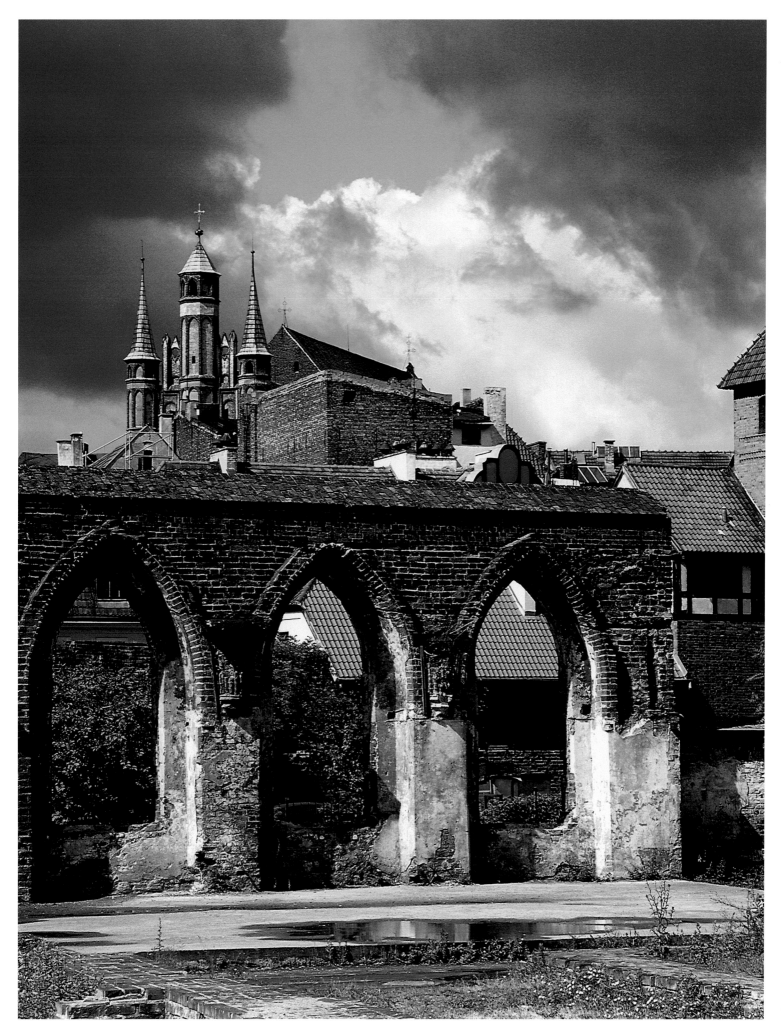

Toruń, one of the most fascinating cities in Poland. The entrance gate
and part of the walls of the no longer extant Church and Monastery of St. Nicholas.

A panorama of Toruń Old Town from across the river.
The night-time illumination shows the splendour of this historic site.

The Gothic Church of St. James
with its characteristic "split" tower.

Monument of Nicolaus Copernicus,
the famous astronomer born and bred in Toruń.

Greater Poland (*Wielkopolska*)
is the cradle of the Polish State.
In 966 Prince Mieszko was
converted to Christianity here,
and in 1000 his son Boleslaus
the Brave hosted the Emperor
Otto III in Gniezno.
Those times are recalled
in the local archaeological
excavations. But Greater Poland
also boasts splendid historic
monuments, palaces, and country
mansions, a rolling countryside
and modern farms.

The Gothic edifice of Gniezno Cathedral. It was erected on the 11th-century foundations of the Romanesque church which went back to the origins of the millennial history of the Metropolitan Archdiocese of Gniezno.

St. Adalbert's reliquary in Gniezno Cathedral. In 1000 AD the Emperor Otto III made a pilgrimage to the tomb of St. Adalbert, Poland's patron.

The late 12th-century Gniezno Door is one of Europe's rarest specimens of Romanesque art. The bas-reliefs present the story of the life and martyrdom of St. Adalbert.

Sunrise over the fields along the River Warta near Rogalinek. Apart from the famous Rogalin Oaks, there are willows here – a typical feature of the Greater Polish countryside.

Biskupińskie Lake. Its western bank is the site of the well-known archaeological reserve, a great tourist attraction.

81

The well-preserved remains of a Lusatian Culture
defensive settlement were discovered at Biskupin
quite by accident in 1933, during a peat-dig.

Kórnik Castle was originally a Renaissance edifice. In the 19th century its proprietor, Tytus Działyński, commissioned Carl Schinkel, a distinguished Berlin architect, to convert it into a Neo-Gothic structure.

The country house at Rogalin was once the residence of the Raczyński family. The beautiful edifice is a combination of Late Baroque and Neo-Classical.

The grounds of Rogalin, and the surrounding fields and meadows
along the Warta contain Europe's largest collection of vintage oaks.
The oldest trees go back nearly 600 years.

Poznań, *regional capital of Greater Poland, is full of historic sites going back to the early days of the Polish State under the Piast dynasty, as well as memorabilia from subsequent times in the development of this important centre for trade and culture. Nowadays Poznań is the venue for Poland's biggest trade fairs, with crowds of visitors from home and abroad.*

Poznań Cathedral stands on the site of the Early Romanesque church erected under the Piast Dynasty, whose first monarchs, Mieszko I and his son Boleslaus the Brave, were buried there.

The Neo-Renaissance building housing
the Aula of the Adam Mickiewicz University, Poznań.

One of the eye-catching architectural features of Poznań's marketplace is the Neo-Classical façade of Działyński House.

The famous Rams of Poznań atop the Town Hall make a special midday tourist attraction.

The opulent Renaissance façade on Poznań's Town Hall,
which owes its decoration to the Italian architect Gianbattista Quadro.

Warsaw: a phoenix rising up out of the ashes. Panorama of the Old Town
with St. John's Cathedral as a special landmark.

Warsaw, *once the seat of the Dukes of Mazovia, and Poland's capital since 1596. "The Unvanquished City" was left virtually a ruin after the Warsaw Uprising (1944), but rose up again and was rebuilt. Today Warsaw is Poland's political and business focus, a place where life takes on a faster, modern perspective.*

The Warsaw Barbakan, originally built in the mid-16th century by Gianbattista Veneziano, as the last stage of the city's defence walls, was fully reconstructed after World War 2.

The Young Insurgent's Memorial. There were no age limits for service during the 1944 Warsaw Uprising, and Varsovians young and old generously offered their lives up for the freedom of their city.

Wilanów Palace, King John Sobieski's French-style suburban residence appointed in a sumptuous Baroque manner and set in splendid grounds.

The Chopin Monument by Wacław Szymanowski, in the Łazienki Park.

The country house at Żelazowa Wola, birthplace of Chopin,
Poland's most famous composer.

The marketplace of Kazimierz Dolny, and next to it the Renaissance Parish Church. Kazimierz grew and prospered as a commercial town on the Vistula river route.

Mikołaj Przybyła's granary. In Kazimierz's heyday there were about three score granaries like this one in the town.

Panorama of Kazimierz from Góra Trzech Krzyży.
The town is a favourite venue for painters, poets, and tourists.

The entrance gate into Lublin's Renaissance royal castle.
The Neo-Gothic edifice replaced the 14th-century medieval fortress.

Zamość Town Hall. This city was founded in 1580 by Lord Chancellor Jan Zamoyski,
and the Italian architect Bernardo Morando designed a well-coordinated Renaissance municipal layout for it.

Picturesque panorama of Sandomierz, a city
with a long and rich history situated on
an escarpment overlooking the Vistula.

Riverside view of Sandomierz Castle. Only one wing
survives of the stronghold erected by Casimir the Great
in the 14th century.

A high attic decorates the 16th-century
Renaissance structure of Sandomierz Town Hall
in the marketplace.

The Puszcza Jodłowa, an ancient forest lovingly described
in the novels of Stefan Żeromski.

In **the Świętokrzyskie Region** *you'll see the low, bare-crested hills; here you can visit the monastery at Święty Krzyż, listen to the rustle of Jodłowa Forest, be charmed by the beautiful historic sites and undulating countryside. There was an early metal industry here; the 18th-century scientist Stanisław Staszic founded an engineering college at Kielce for the mining and metallurgical industries.*

Łysicia, the highest peak in the Góry Świętokrzyskie (Holy Cross Mountains); view from Psary-Podlasie.

Jaskinia Raj – the "Paradise Cave" – is one of Poland's most spectacular places for stalactites and stalagmites.

Zagnańsk: the famous Bartek Oak,
which goes back to the Middle Ages.

Oh, what can be finer than those tall, tall trees
Wrought in sunset's bronze by the evening light,
Over water reflecting deep the tumbling panoplies
Of branches rippled by colours bright.

Leopold Staff
1878–1957

Kielce: the towers of the Cathedral and former Bishop's Palace
rising over the city's castle hill.

The Jewish cemetery at Ożarów is a memorial
to the community that once lived in the locality.

Ruins of the metallurgical works at Samsonów.
In the 19th century there was a modern blast furnace here.

109

The Valley of the Pokrzywianka.
A summer storm's drawing up.

Krzyżtopór Castle at Ujazd. The once magnificent residence of the Ossoliński family was devastated during the mid-17th -century Swedish Wars.

Wąchock Abbey, a Cistercian foundation and one of Poland's finest specimens of Romanesque architecture.

Ruins of Chęciny Castle, a medieval royal residence, once the venue for conventions
of knights of the realm and the place where the royal treasury was kept.

The Valley of the Opatówka: with a country river and willows on its banks,
it looks just like a romantic idyll.

The windmill at Krasocin, a place in the Kielce region, dates back to the 19th century and is well-nigh symbolic of the rural countryside.

Sunrise over Opatów Collegiate Church. This Romanesque basilica has had several conversions, but still it retains some of its earliest features.

The Neo-Classical *dwór* country house at Nagłowice, on the site of the old residence of Mikołaj Rej, a 16th-century writer referred to as the father of Polish literature.

Late Baroque country mansion at Czyżów Szlachecki, on the site of a medieval castle.

117

Jędrzejów Cistercian Church, erected in the 13th century
and later converted in a Baroque style.

Colourful fields and meadows with a faint outline of hills on the horizon
– that's the landscape of the Polish uplands.

Wrocław, *regional capital of Lower Silesia (Dolny Śląsk), lies on the Oder and its tributaries. It's a charming city of islands and bridges. A bishop's see already in the 11th century, Wrocław has numerous historic sites, especially on Ostrów Tumski Island.*
The patricians' heritage is represented by Wrocław's fine Renaissance town hall and the houses round its marketplace.

Wrocław. The Tumski Bridge joins Piaskowa Island with Ostrów Tumski Island, marked by the sharp spires of its Gothic Cathedral.

The Młyński Bridge on Piaskowa Island. Wrocław owes some of its special charm to its unusual location.

The richly decorated masonry on the east elevation
of Wrocław's Late Gothic Town Hall.

The Aula Leopoldina in Wrocław University:
a masterpiece of Baroque art.

Ostrów Tumski,
the island where Wrocław's history began.

A splendid view of the Collegiate Church
of the Holy Cross from the botanical gardens.

The mighty Książ Castle near Wałbrzych, once the seat of the Dukes of Silesia,
and later of the Hochberg family.

125

Czocha Castle, a Gothic edifice in Poland's south-western corner, converted in the early 20th century (after a fire) on the basis of 18th-century Baroque building plans.

Sunrise over Śnieżka, the highest summit
in the Karkonosze and Sudetan Mountains.

The Sudetan Mountain Range *runs along the Polish-Czech border. It consists of several groups and chains, of which the best-known are the Karkonosze, the Góry Stołowe, and the Śnieżnik Massif. Their gently rounded tops neighbour on steep slopes, dangerous precipices, and unusually shaped rock formations.*

The Śnieżne Stawki tarns in the kettle Śnieżne Kotły, in the western part of the Karkonosze Mountains.

Autumn mists over Równia, near Śnieżka Mountain.

The slopes of Kocioł Małego Stawu with a scenic waterfall.
The sun endows the rocks with ecstatic colours.

Słonecznik rock is over 12 m high. Unusual rock formations are a typical feature of Karkonosze and Sudetan landscapes.

Fairy-tale landscape of snow-clad island mountains.

The Karkonosze forests under a cap of snow
and hoar-frost.

132

The Pauline Monastery at Jasna Góra. Częstochowa is the principal Polish place
of pilgrimage for the cult of the Virgin Mary.

The Chapel of Our Lady Queen of Poland, Jasna Góra.
The people of Poland hold the Black Madonna in special reverence.

135

Main nave of Wawel Cathedral with the Confession
of St. Stanislaus, Bishop and Martyr, Patron of Poland.

I have a land, the country of my spirit,
There my heart keeps many bosom kindred;
Fairest are the sights that lie within it,
Dearer its fellows than my blood familiars.

Thither from cares and toil, thither from play
Fleeing, where by the pine-trees unhurried sit I,
'Mid fragrant herbs there passing the day,
But sparrows chasing, and catching butterflies.

Adam Mickiewicz
1798–1855

Cracow is a city of churches and historic sites, a cultural centre, a magical destination for visitors from home and abroad, all drawn up by its singular atmosphere. There's Wawel Castle and Cathedral, with the royal crypt of the kings of Poland, museums, galleries, vestiges of the Jewish culture of Kazimierz . . .
I could go on and on . . .

Cracow's Market Square, one of Europe's biggest medieval marketplace. The Gothic tower is all that's left of the town hall, which was demolished in the 19th century. Next to it is the corner of the Cloth Hall.

Wawel Hill, around which historic Cracow grew up, and on which the kings of Poland had their principal residence.

139

Ulica Kanonicza, one of Cracow's prettiest streets,
with a vista onto the bastion of the Royal Castle
and the Cathedral towers.

The Adam Mickiewicz Monument was erected in 1898, as a tribute for the centenary of the poet's birth.

The towers of the Gothic edifice of St. Mary's Basilica, It's from here that the bugle is sounded every hour.

141

Interior of St. Mary's, with polychromies by Jan Matejko
and the Veit Stoss Main Altar.

The Juliusz Słowacki Theatre (formerly the Municipal Theatre) opened in 1893. Its characteristically Cracovian edifice was designed by Jan Zawiejski.

The Planty Gardens, an extraordinary park encircling Cracow's Old Town, were founded on the site of the old fortifications.

Wawel Castle: the Hen's Foot and the Gothic Pavilion,
remnants of the medieval castle blending into
the Renaissance structures.

The Old Synagogue in the Kazimierz district of Cracow, built in the 16th century after a design by Matteo Gucci.

The sumptuous interior of the Tempel Synagogue, with an architecture clearly reminiscent of the Mauretanian style.

The *almemor* or *bima* (pulpit) in the central prayer
hall of the Old Synagogue.

The Baroque gate leading up to Skałka Pauline Church and the pool known as "Poland's holy water bowl" into which, according to legend, the body of St. Stanislaus was thrown.

Corpus Christi Church, founded in 1340 by Casimir the Great.
Today its Gothic structure stands on one of the corners of plac Wolnica.

The famous Wieliczka Salt Mine. Its tourist route takes you through
the ancient corridors and chambers in the mine, and is traversed
by over 700 thousand visitors every year.

Salt has been extracted here for thousands of years.
Already by 3,000 B. C. there were brine evaporation works here;
while the first mine shafts were dug much later by Benedictine monks.

Fragments of matzevah tombstones make up a local
Wailing Wall in the Remuh Cemetery
in the Kazimierz quarter of Cracow.

Tombstones
in the Jewish Remuh Cemetery.
Vestiges of a massacred culture.

The former Auschwitz-Birkenau concentration camp, now a memorial museum, near the city of Oświęcim. This place is a memorial to unimaginable genocide, a warning for future generations.

Lesser Poland (*Małopolska*)

*was once the central
region of Poland.
This was where
aristocratic courtiers
built their castles,
where monasteries
and pilgrimage centres
sprang up, along with
important towns.
So there's plenty to see,
as well as the fine,
differentiated landscape.*

The Observantine Monastery at Kalwaria Zebrzydowska, a place of pilgrimage for the cult of the Virgin Mary. This open-air Calvary shrine, the best-known one in Poland, was founded in the early 17th century by Mikołaj Zebrzydowski.

Wiśnicz Castle, a Gothic/Renaissance structure, was once the residence of the aristocratic Kmita and Lubomirski families.

The Benedictine Abbey at Tyniec on the outskirts of Cracow,
is one of the oldest religious foundations in Poland. King Boleslaus
the Bold is believed to have been its founder (in the 11th century).

Visitors come to Zalipie, an extraordinary village near Tarnów,
to admire the stunning floral painted decorations on the cottages.

Brightly coloured posies sparkle
on every cottage.

Not only do the womenfolk of Zalipie decorate the walls of their cottages, but also their household and kitchen appliances.

Łańcut Castle near Rzeszów, In the 18th and 19th centuries the old fortress
was converted into a magnificent stately residence.

The 18th-century Church of the Discovery of the Holy Cross is the central place
of worship at Kalwaria Pacławska, a Calvary shrine near Przemyśl.

The Neo-Classical *dwór* country cottage at Bolestraszyce,
once owned by painter Piotr Michałowski, is located in a park of exotic trees.

Panorama of the Old Town of Przemyśl, a picturesque border city of many churches, cultures, and religions, and proud of its thousand years of history.

Sub-Carpathia (*Podkarpacie*)
is borderland country,
a kaleidoscope of many
cultures, religions,
and traditions.
History has not been kind
here, with numerous episodes
of invasion and devastation.
Despite this there are still
plenty of fascinating places,
which, coupled with
the splendid landscape,
make Sub-Carpathia
an exciting region

162

Krasiczyn Castle was erected at the turn of the 16th
and 17th centuries by Jakub and Stanisław Krasicki.

The River San near Bachów in the Przemyśl
Foothills Natural Landscape Park.

A cottage in the Sanok open-air museum, the largest collection of exhibits showing the Polish folk building crafts.

Ulucz Church is one of the finest wooden Eastern-Rite places of worship in Sub-Carpathia.

Extant part of Sanok Castle,
a Gothic/Renaissance structure.

166

The San, the largest and extremely scenic river
in south-east Poland.

I'd cast down everything and return
To the little town where I was born,

. . .

Along the riverside where willows grow,
By shallow waters I'd abscond,
In harmless search afar to go,
The ever-wandering vagabond.

Kazimierz Wierzyński
1894–1969

For years **the Bieszczady Mountains** have been fascinating tourists: both the boating fans heading for Lake Solińskie, and the enthusiasts of the wild, well-nigh primal countryside, where they can see the ruins of deserted villages, admire the scenic river gorges, and wander off into the połonina mountains.

170

The Bieszczady and Low Beskid Mountains are a land of wooden churches – like this Eastern-Rite one in the village of Jałowe – small and beautiful.

The Cottage on the Połonina Wetlińska, the mountain shelter at the highest altitude in the Bieszczady Mountains.

Równia Eastern-Rite Church, mid-18th-century,
one of the finest in the Bieszczady Mountains.

The Połonina Caryńska with Tarnica in the distance. The Bieszczady Mountains are famous for the *połoniny*, their high-altitude meadows.

The Hylaty mountain river at the foot of the summit Dwernik Kamień.

Picturesque rapids on the Wetlinka.

Waterfall on a woodland stream near Wetlina.

Sails on Lake Solińskie. This artificial lake was created when a dam was built on the River San. In summer hundreds of holidaymakers and sailing enthusiasts come here.

The Beskidy Mountains are a scenic part of Poland. Nature lovers come here for the varied landscapes, rich wildlife and historic sites.

Picturesque valleys and remote villages lie amid the not very high Beskid Sądecki Hills.

Environs of Rytro and the road for Niemcowa in the Beskid Sądecki Hills
Rytro has the ruins of a castle in its locality, and lies in the gorge of the Poprad Valley.

Niedzica Castle, a medieval knights' residence. At the turn of the 16th and 17th centuries it was owned by the Hungarian Horwath family. Today it rises spectacularly over the waters in the Czorsztyn Dam.

The Podhalanian village of Chochołów, with extant wooden architecture from the turn of the 19th and 20th centuries.

The Tatras are Poland's highest mountains, majestic and formidable, a part of the Western Carpathians.
The small section of the Tatras within Poland's borders is enough to make you wonder at their might, and charm you with the view of their snow-capped peaks or with the highland folk music. You won't want to leave.

The *regiel* sub-alpine woodlands in the environs of the valley Dolina Kościeliska.

Dolina Kościeliska, considered the most beautiful valley in the Tatras, with an easy hiking route along it.

The tarn Czarny Staw near Lake Morskie Oko,
with the slopes of Mięguszowieckie Szczyty beyond.

The kettle containing Lake Morskie Oko and the tarn Czarny Staw, near Rysy Mountain. The other peaks (from left to right) are Żabi Koń, Wołowy Grzbiet, and Mięguszowieckie Szczyty.

Villa Koliba, the first house built in the Zakopane Style after a design by Stanisław Witkiewicz.

Since the 19th century the magic of the Tatras has been exciting visitors
with the majesty and beauty of the mountains, giving those who dare climb
them a sense of power and the thrill of adventure.

The majestic peak Mięguszowiecki Szczyt Wielki,
with Lodowy and Łomnica beyond.

A panorama of Buczynowe Turnie,
the Bielsko Tatras and the High Tatras from Orla Baszta.

189

Environs of the Valley of the Five Polish Tarns (*Dolina Pięciu Stawów Polskich*),
with Hruby and Krywań in the background: the power and awe of the mountains.

View from Mięguszowiecki Szczyt Czarny, with the ridge between Żabie Szczyty and Kopa Spadowa in the foreground, marking the frontier between Poland and Slovakia. Our expedition has come to an end . . .

38-622 Olszanica 311
Office: 38-600 Lesko, ul. Parkowa 5
tel. +48 (13) 4699000
tel./fax +48 (13) 4696188
e-mail: biuro@bosz.com.pl
www.bosz.com.pl

Price 59 zł